GILLIAN WOLFE is Director, Learning and Public Affairs,
at Dulwich Picture Gallery (one of the most renowned private collections
in the UK) and has been Head of Education there since 1984.
Her children's art books include *My First Art Book*, winner of
the Parent Choice Silver Honour Award in the USA; and *Art Activity*
and *Children's Art Book*, both winners of the Gulbenkian Prize
for the best Museum Publications of the Year.
LOOK! Zoom in on Art! also published by Frances Lincoln,
was the winner of the English Association's 4-11 award for the best
non-fiction book. In was followed by the very popular
LOOK! Body Language in Art.

In 1995 Gillian was awarded the MBE and in 2000 a CBE for Services
to Art Education. She is a Fellow of the Royal Society of Art.

textured

dappled misty rainy

cold dramatic milky

candlelight sparkling

rainbow natural

foggy limpid gleamin

stormy silvery dull

dotty spotlight flashing

glowing metalic

hot steamy icy bright

rosy smokey twinkling

flickering

searchlight mellow

electric creepy

coloured

moonlight cloudy

pearly reflected

natural

cold

candlelight

dramatic

rainy

twinkling

icy

spotlight

coloured

moonlight

milky

flickering

rosy

limpid

foggy

sparkling

smokey

reflected

rainbow

mellow

gleaming

flashing

pearly

dappled

cloudy

hot

bright

silvery

metalic

creepy

stormy

electric

dotty

steamy

searchlight

glowing

misty

dull

textured

LOOK!

Seeing the Light in Art

Gillian Wolfe

FRANCES LINCOLN
CHILDREN'S BOOKS

To Caryl Hubbard, for her wisdom and loyal support.

PHOTOGRAPHIC ACKNOWLEDGMENTS

For permission to reproduce the works of art on the following pages and for supplying
photographs, the Publishers would like to thank:

Bridgeman Art Library (www.bridgeman.co.uk): back cover and 22–3, 14, 16–17, 26–7, 38–9
Reproduced by kind permission of the Dan Dare Corporation Limited: 32–3
By permission of the Trustees of Dulwich Picture Gallery, London: 12, 19
© 2005 The M.C. Escher Company-Holland. All rights reserved. www.mcescher.com: 21
Photo © 1999 The Metropolitan Museum of Art: cover and 24–5 (The Mr and Mrs Charles Kramer Collection,
Gift of Mr and Mrs Charles Kramer, 1979. 1979.620.90/© Succession Picasso/DACS 2006)
Courtesy DC Moore Gallery, NYC: 36 (Collection: Samuel Harn Museum of Art, Gainesville, FL)
Museo Casa Diego Rivera, Guanajuato, México: 13 (© 2005 Banco de México, Diego Rivera &
Frida Kahlo Museums Trust, Av. Cinco de Mayo No.2, Col.Centro, Del. Cuauhtémoc 06059, México, D.F./INBAL)
Digital image © 2005 The Museum of Modern Art, New York/Scala, Florence: 10–11 (Gift of Mrs Simon Guggenheim. 646.1939)
Rijksmuseum, Amsterdam: 30–1
The Royal Collection © 2006, Her Majesty Queen Elizabeth II: 34–5
© Photo Scala, Florence: 8–9
© Tate, London (2006): 4–5, 18, 28–9 (reproduced by permission of the Henry Moore Foundation)

Look! Seeing the Light in Art copyright © Frances Lincoln Limited 2006
Text copyright © Gillian Wolfe 2006

First published in Great Britain in 2006 and in the USA in 2007
by Frances Lincoln Children's Books, 4 Torriano Mews,
Torriano Avenue, London NW5 2RZ

www.franceslincoln.com

First paperback published in Great Britain in 2009 and in the USA in 2010

British Library Cataloguing in Publication Data available on request

ISBN 978-1-84780-038-1

Printed in Singapore

1 3 5 7 9 8 6 4 2

Contents

Look at **dramatic** light

Have you ever been to the theatre and seen the way spotlights highlight the action on stage? Long before stage lights were invented this artist used dramatic lighting to make his paintings more powerful. This painting demands your attention. It certainly is a very unusual scene.

Saint Paul sprawls awkwardly on the ground under the raised leg of a hefty-looking horse. He has been overcome by a vision so powerful that he has completely lost control.

Deep shadows surround the brilliantly lit action. Look at the way light catches Paul's outspread fingers. Light hits the long vein in the old man's leg and highlights the smooth curves of the patient horse. Saint Paul is painted upside down and pushed right up against the edge of the picture-frame. His feet seem to be a long way away but his arms and hands are close up, vividly bright and startling.

Dramatic lighting makes this an unforgettable picture. No wonder this artist has been called 'Master of Light'.

For drama, use white chalk to highlight important parts of your drawing. Add deep shadows with dark chalks around the highlighted parts.

Caravaggio, *The Conversion of St Paul*

Look at **mysterious** light

Are you puzzled by this picture? Perhaps the lion is puzzled too. He doesn't look at all dangerous. He seems curious. The lion has discovered a gypsy asleep on the sand.

The moon gives out a strangely magical light. Rousseau has highlighted the lion's eyes and toes and

individual hairs on the lion's mane and tail. He cleverly paints the light side of the girl's stick as another stripe of colour in her dress. The strings of her mandolin echo the dress stripes. Some people think this picture has a childlike feel about it, others wonder if it might be a painting of a dream. How would *you* explain the mystery?

Around the lion and the sleeping gypsy, the silky smooth sand is quite undisturbed. There are no footprints, so how did they get there?

Draw what happens next when the gypsy wakes up to find a lion watching her in the moonlight!

Henri Rousseau, *The Sleeping Gypsy*

Look at **cold** and **hot** light

It's freezing and something important is happening. Villagers are preparing to kill a pig. When snow and ice covered the land, food was scarce.

How has Teniers captured a completely icy feel? For this cold look Teniers used all sorts of silvery-grey colours. Hold a piece of white paper against the picture. Is any of the painting actually white? Look for the few places where he uses white for brilliant highlights?

David Teniers the Younger, *A Winter's Scene with a Man Killing a Pig*

Diego Rivera, *La Era*

Farming in a hot dry country like Mexico is very hard work. Blue and purple colours show the cold light of the distant mountain peaks, where little can grow. Below them, the bright greens show a valley lush with crops. Nearest to us are the scorching colours of dry, baked earth.

This painting seems to burn with heat. Only the cool of the mountains gives any relief. How can you tell from which direction the sun is shining?

Design a seasons calendar. Think about which scene and colours will go best with spring, summer, autumn and winter.

Look at **dappled** light

You may think that this picture is about a girl on a swing but it is really about light.

Sunshine darts between leaves. It makes light patches and light splashes in the shady clearing among the trees. Light flickers over the man's back. Light plays over the woman's dress. A light and shade mixture like this is called *dappled*.

People are outdoors, relaxing in the park on a beautiful day in Paris. You get a feeling of hazy light and shimmering colours. Renoir was trying to show the way light dances over the human body.

Renoir was one of a group of artists called the Impressionists. They had to paint fast to capture the constantly changing light in different sorts of weather. They also had to cope with a few insects flying into their oil paint!

Dappled sunlight is excellent camouflage for forest creatures. Make your own picture where animals with spots, stripes and patches merge in the dappled shade.

Pierre Auguste Renoir, *The Swing*

Look at rainy light

What a downpour! Have you ever had a soaking like this? Battered by a torrent of rain, seven people race for shelter. Three of them huddle under one umbrella, another protects himself with a mat. They run, bent over, against the fierce rain, hardly able to see where they are going.

Trees on the distant shore are deliberately made to look misty. This adds to the impression of seeing them through a haze of rain. Heavy black clouds block out the sun.

Hundreds of thin criss-crossing lines of rain slant across the picture adding to the gloomy light. Pale grey lines were cleverly printed underneath black ones to give a more naturally rainy effect.

What might happen if the sun suddenly shines through the rain? Make a glorious rainbow across your own rainy picture to cheer up all your wet people.

Hiroshige Ando, *Sudden Shower on Ohashi Bridge at Atake*

Look at **stormy** and **calm** light

Snow, sea, wind and sky whirl together in a violent storm. You can just see the mast of a fragile steamboat. Look at the black smoke from its funnel and follow it with your finger as it twists and blows into the storm clouds.

The artist was on that boat. Tied to the mast, he watched the stormy light for four hours so he could paint it in his studio later. Don't you think he must have been very brave?

Joseph Mallord William Turner, *Snow Storm – Steam-Boat off a Harbour's Mouth*

Aelbert Cuyp, *A Road Near a River*

Next time the sun goes down, stand and look at the shadows cast by your body. In this painting, long thin evening shadows stretch right across the road. This artist has painted the most delicate sky – there are no fiery red colours here. An almost *secret* sunset hides just around the corner, shedding a pearly golden light over the countryside.

Would you choose the calm of a gentle sunset or the excitement of a wild storm? Draw yourself in the type of scene you would prefer.

Look at reflected light

Can you guess why this picture is called *Three Worlds*? Above the water the trees live in the land world. What we see is their reflection in the water.

Leaves float on the top of a watery world. Because water has a sort of skin, they can lie there. Have you ever seen a water-boatman insect skim across the surface of the water in the same way?

Below the water is another world, deep and dark. The handsome fish lives in that secret world.

All shiny surfaces reflect light. When you look in a mirror you see what you look like because light reflects your face back in the glass. Water reflects light. Look in a puddle and see your reflection. Throw a stone into the puddle and watch your reflection shatter into rippling patterns.

If you looked into this pond, would your reflection stare back at you alongside the fish?

Look at the pictures in this book and find other examples of where light is reflected. Name all the types of surfaces which are good and bad for reflecting light.

Maurits Cornelius Escher, *Three Worlds*

Look at light **patterns**

Have you ever looked at light coming through a window and noticed how it makes a pattern on the wall?

This is a room in Egypt. Girls wearing beautiful costumes are trying on jewellery. A decorated screen against the window helps to reduce the fierce glare of the sun. Sunlight streams in through the gaps in the screen. Rays of light carry the screen decoration on to the wall in a diagonal design.

Can you see how this delicate light pattern travels across the face and hand of the resting girl. It spreads across her leg to the couch and spills on to the floor. You can imagine the sweltering heat, the buzzing flies, and girls being too hot to move quickly in their heavy clothes.

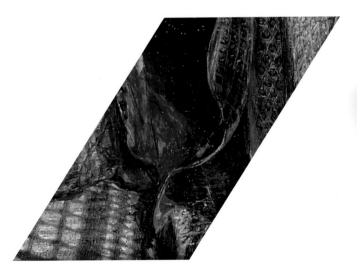

How many shadow patterns can you make with your hands? Try to spot three different light patterns around you today.

John Frederick Lewis, *Indoor Gossip, Cairo*

Pablo Picasso, *Still Life by Lamplight*

Look at light shapes

Picasso's paintings show us a new way of looking at shapes. Many artists have spent a lifetime perfecting the technique of gently merging light and dark. Picasso breaks the rules and does the opposite. All the light and shade in this picture has been deliberately captured and enclosed in shapes.

Lamplight flares out and swirls around into the darkness. Bright yellow patterns dance under the light bulb where the light is strongest. Long ribbons of darker shapes stream off around the room. These deeper shades seem to be escaping from the bright intense centre of light.

Look at the shadows cast by the apples on the table's surface. These are carefully outlined to give each shadow its own precise shape.

Can you see a tiny white star where the lamplight hits the edge of the glass? This is a humorous way of showing a sparkle.

Picasso did not actually see these shapes – he made them up. The shapes add movement and excitement. Show light and dark like this in your own shape picture.

Vincent van Gogh, *Road with Cypress and Star*

Look at light **textures**

Vincent van Gogh loved cypress trees.
He said they were a splash of black in a sunny landscape.
This huge tree splits the sky into two halves – one side
lit by stars and the other by the moon.

Two men walk home after a hard day. A horse-drawn
cart with huge wooden wheels trundles after
them. Yet the people hardly matter
because all the drama is in the sky.

This is no ordinary summer night.
A brilliant halo of light surrounds the
golden star, making it appear to spin
and vibrate. We often think of the
moon as pale and silvery,
but van Gogh's moon
almost burns with crusty
textured yellow and orange.
His excited brushstrokes give a wild
feel to the luminous sky. It looks as if he
painted fast and furiously. His thick strokes
of glowing colour gives the surface a rich and
craggy feel.

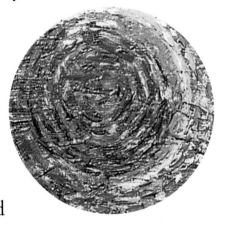

Let your imagination run
wild. Make fantastic stars,
suns and moons in glorious colours
with thick, textured paint.

Look at light **lines**

Henry Moore, *Pink and Green Sleepers*

These people are trying to get a good night's sleep.
It isn't easy. The city around them is filled with the terrifying
noise of aeroplanes on a bombing raid. This is London in wartime.

For protection, many people rushed into the underground train
stations at night. They made up beds on the hard platforms and
tried to sleep as best they could. It must have been very uncomfortable.

Henry Moore was a sculptor, famous for making massive stone figures. He drew the people he saw wrapped up in their bedding in the tunnels. He thought their shapes looked like sculptures.

When you look at Henry Moore's drawings you can see that his figures almost stand out of the page. Look at the way the artist draws lines that wrap around the arms. Each line goes right round the body. More delicate lines show the shape of the fingers and face.

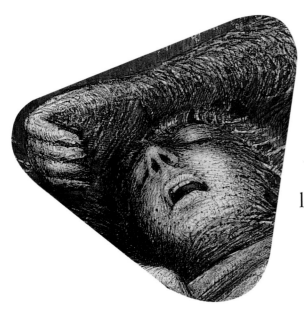

Wax crayons make lines that glide over and around the shapes. Wax is shiny and catches the light. It is greasy and cannot easily be covered over by paint. Because of this, wax makes a lovely broken texture.

Make a magic picture using thick crayons. Brush all over the picture with thin paint. Watch as the paint refuses to cover the wax lines.

29

Look at light **solids**

Just look at this magnificent head. You feel as if you could almost put your hands around the man's turban and lift it up! Bulging folds of cloth makes an imposing headdress. The texture of the material looks soft, yet the shape appears sturdy. The centre of the turban is lit by brilliant highlights. It seems to swell up and almost burst out of the picture. Rembrandt is a master of shading. His people almost loom out of the deep shadows, their faces looking lit up and alive. Light and dark are skilfully blended. Your eye is deceived into thinking that a flat shape is actually solid. The smooth change from dense shade to intense light happens so gradually you are hardly aware of it.

Draw the outline of a bowl then draw it again. This time add gentle shading around the edges. Which drawing looks the most solid?

Rembrandt, *Head of a Man in Oriental Costume*

Look at light **contrasts**

Frank Hampson, *Dan Dare, Pilot of the Future*

This is Dan Dare, space pilot with a mission. His job is to search out and destroy any aliens planning to invade Earth.

The gripping adventures of this science fiction hero became known to millions of children in a strip cartoon. It was on the front cover of the weekly *Eagle* comic.

The artwork was exquisite and the colours looked good because of the high quality printing.

Frank Hampson wanted to capture the sense of space travel. With the advice of a space expert, he built models of spaceships. That way he could get the light and shade contrasts exactly right. Look at how he captures the shine of light gleaming on metal, plastic and skin. He does this by making bold contrasts of colour.

The artist shows deep shadows as solid black shapes. His highlights are white. Try drawing a face with striking contrast, like this.

33

Sir Edwin Landseer, *Isaac van Amburgh and his Animals*

Look at highlights

Isaac van Amburgh was a lion-tamer who thrilled the public by giving performances both outdoors and in London theatres.

In this painting the cage is like a dark cave, and we seem to be inside it looking out through the bars at the spectators.

Parts of each animal are highlighted to make them stand out. They almost glow inside the gloomy cave. Look at the way light catches the tiger's head. His wet mouth and dangerous teeth gleam, his whiskers and fur shine. The tiger's claws look frighteningly real. Did those claws have something to do with the red scratches on van Amburgh's arm and neck? Perhaps the animals were not always so friendly after all!

Queen Victoria was so excited by his daring show that she went to see it five times and even wrote about it in her diary.

Use the lioness's gleaming eye as an example. Draw eyes that come alive with highlights like this.

Yvonne Jacquette, *Tokyo Street with Pachinko Parlor II*

Look at **night** lights

Brilliant neon lights flood the whole street.
Look at the road surface, pavements, buses and cars.
They all glow with intense reflected colour. Short strokes
of bright paint almost look like thread and give an
impression of a multicoloured woven fabric.

Vivid lights add warmth and energy to this bustling
scene in Tokyo City, Japan. A massive building is almost
entirely covered with lights to attract as much attention
as possible. It dominates the picture and dwarfs everything.
The artist has painted the view from high up in another
tall building. You feel as if you are looking down on little
stick people and toy cars.

The twinkling lettering of the signs and advertisements
encourages people to stay out late and be a part of the
nightlife. They say that cities never sleep. Electric light
makes that possible. Lights keep the dark at bay.
Nightlights turn night into day.

Make the brightest colours you
possibly can. Try them out on
dark paper, and then on white paper.
Which colours glow the most?

Look at **heavenly** light

Brilliant gold rays of light
pour into a garden so beautiful that
it looks like Paradise. Two angels kneel
in the glowing rays. They hold up their
hands as if to warm themselves.

This artist was not painting the weather.
He wanted light to mean something.
Circles of bright holy light surround the
heads of all the people. They hold hands,
showing that there is only love and peace
in the garden.

Have you ever heard someone say that
they have 'seen the light'? What they really mean is that
they have understood something. The golden shaft of light
bathing the angels means the light of understanding.

Gold used to be the most special
of all colours. It reflected the gleam
from candlelight and was only used
for very important pictures.

Look at the front and back
pages of this book to find
lots of words describing light.
Can you think of any more?

Fra Angelico, *Paradise from The Last Judgment*

Look it up

Here you can find out more about the art and artists in this book, including when the paintings were made, when the artists lived, and where you can see the paintings.

Pages 8–9
The Conversion of St Paul, 1600–01
Caravaggio (1573–1610)
Santa Maria del Popolo, Rome, Italy

Caravaggio's paintings were criticised in his lifetime. He was not afraid to paint ordinary people as they really were, including their grubby clothes and dirty feet. His dramatic use of light and shade was a new way of painting that astonished people. Caravaggio had a wild and violent personality; he was often imprisoned and on the run from the law.

Pages 10–11
The Sleeping Gypsy, 1897
Henri Rousseau (1844–1910)
The Museum of Modern Art, New York, USA

Rousseau, a French artist, worked as a customs officer in France. When he was 40 he taught himself to paint in his spare time. Later, he ran a school for art, drama, and music. Rousseau's paintings have a haunting, dreamlike quality, as if they are scenes from another world.

Page 12
A Winter's Scene with a Man Killing a Pig, c. 1650
David Teniers the Younger (1610–90)
Dulwich Picture Gallery, London, UK

David Teniers the Younger came from a family of artists. His father and son were also artists and also called David so there is often confusion about who painted what. He painted every possible kind of picture including peasant scenes, landscapes, portraits, and animal pictures. He painted over 2000 pictures, and his best works are those made before he was 40.

Page 13
La Era, 1904
Diego Rivera (1886–1957)
Diego Rivera Museum, Guanajuato, Mexico

A Mexican artist with strong opinions about politics, Rivera's artwork is bold and colourful. European painters and Aztec Indian art from South America influenced his style. He made massive wall paintings (murals) about revolution. He wanted everyone, especially the Mexican poor, to be able to see and understand the messages in his art.

Page 14
The Swing, 1876
Pierre Auguste Renoir (1841–1919)
The Louvre, Paris, France

Renoir began work at the age of 13 in a china factory painting porcelain. All his life he loved visiting art galleries to study the work of the great painters. He joined the artists called the Impressionists. They painted outside to capture the effects of light and shade. Later he concentrated on the human body and brilliantly captured flesh-tones in warm, glowing colours.

Pages 16–17
Sudden Shower on Ohashi Bridge at Ataka
from the series *100 Views of Edo*, 1857
Hiroshige Ando (1797–1858)
Galerie Janette Ostier, Paris, France

Hiroshige was born in Edo, now called Tokyo, the capital of Japan. His landscapes capture well-known scenes that ordinary Japanese people loved. He made many prints to show a single view in all its moods and weather conditions. Hiroshige also created designs for advertisements, fans, envelopes, board games, and book illustrations. Altogether he made over 5000 designs.

Page 18
Snow Storm – Steam-Boat off a Harbour's Mouth, 1842
Joseph Mallord William Turner (1775–1851)
Tate Britain, London, UK

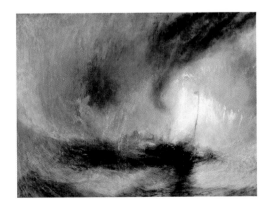

Turner was the son of a London barber. As a child genius, he went to art school aged 14. When he was 21 he went abroad on his first sketching tour and continued to travel and paint for almost fifty years. His later pictures capture magical light effects in pale, brilliant colours. It depressed him to part with his pictures and he often refused to sell them. He is one of the most famous British painters.

Page 19
A Road Near a River, *c.* 1660
Aelbert Cuyp (1620–1691)
Dulwich Picture Gallery, London, UK

Cuyp painted sea pictures, portraits, still life, animal pictures, and especially landscapes. He became fascinated by light effects, in particular how to capture the golden glow of sunlight using light and shade. When he was 40 he married a rich widow and abandoned painting for the last 25 years of his life.

Page 21
Three Worlds, 1955
Maurits Cornelius Escher (1898–1972)
The M.C. Escher Company, The Netherlands

Escher is one of the most original and skilled print-makers. His clever and complicated compositions, often in black, white and grey, appear to trick the eye. His compositions use perspective and architecture in a way that defies the mind and gravity unlike any other artist. Escher said himself that he seemed to have more in common with mathematicians than with other artists.

Pages 22–23
Indoor Gossip, Cairo, 1873
John Frederick Lewis (1805–76)
Whitworth Art Gallery, Manchester, UK

Early in his career, John Frederick Lewis mainly painted animals and sporting subjects with his friend, the artist Sir Edwin Landseer. Later he painted landscape figures and indoor scenes. He travelled a great deal to copy great paintings to develop his own skill. For a while he lived in Spain and then Egypt. On his return to London he became a very successful painter.

Pages 24–25
Still Life by Lamplight, 1962
Pablo Picasso (1881–1973)
The Metropolitan Museum of Art, New York, USA

Picasso, a Spanish artist, changed forever how we understand modern art. He constantly experimented with new ideas and techniques. Picasso developed a new and daring printing method in which if even one mistake is made, the whole piece is ruined. He created many paintings, drawings, collages, prints, ceramics and sculptures during his long lifetime.

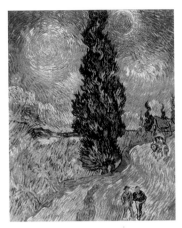

Pages 26–27
Road with Cypress and Star, 1890
Vincent van Gogh (1853–90)
Kroller-Muller Museum, Otterlo, The Netherlands

Van Gogh, a Dutch artist, is one of the most famous painters of all time. He has an energetic painting style using brilliant colours and textured brush stokes. He was not successful in his lifetime and was extremely poor. Many of his pictures are bright, joyful and full of passionate expression, yet they disguise a deeply tormented personality.

Pages 28–29
Pink and Green Sleepers, 1941
Henry Moore (1898–1986)
The Trustees of the Tate Gallery, London, UK

Even as a child Henry Moore knew he wanted to be a sculptor. He is most famous for his sculptures of mother and child, and family groups. His constant interest was always the human body made in stone or bronze. As a war artist he captured the plight of ordinary Londoners sheltering from the bombs in Underground stations.

Pages 30–31
Head of a Man in Oriental Costume, 1635
Rembrandt (1606–69)
Rijksmuseum, Amsterdam, The Netherlands

Rembrandt was the son of a Dutch miller. By the age of 22 he was already acknowledged as brilliant and was teaching his own students. Early on he was successful and became wealthy, but he got into debt so his wife and son had to manage his money. Rembrandt painted 60 self-portraits at each stage of his life showing his gradual aging and increasing sadness. Today, his portraits are famous masterpieces.

Pages 32–33
Dan Dare, Pilot of the Future
from the *Eagle* (Hutton Press), 1959
Frank Hampson (1918–1985)
Private Collection

Frank Hampson wanted to be a pilot, but trained as an illustrator. He hated the horror comics that were flooding the market and set out to offer a quality comic for boys. His beautifully illustrated and gripping stories based on his famous space hero, Dan Dare, sold a million copies of the *Eagle* comic book every week.

Pages 34–35
Isaac van Amburgh and his Animals, 1839
Sir Edwin Landseer (1803–73)
The Royal Collection, London, UK

Landseer's brilliant art career began at the age of 12 when he exhibited his first painting at the Royal Academy. His clever way of giving animals, especially dogs, human expressions, made him extremely popular. He was Queen Victoria's favourite painter.

Page 36
Tokyo Street with Pachinko Parlor II, 1985
Yvonne Jacquette (born 1934)
Samuel Harn Museum, Florida, USA

Yvonne Jacquette shows how the world looks from above. She paints the views from high-rise buildings and aeroplanes. Her pictures are of daytime and nighttime scenes of cities, factories, farmlands, harbours, rivers and roads. She vividly captures the state of the modern landscape with all its energy, confusion, and excitement.

Pages 38–39
Paradise from the Last Judgement, *c. 1430*
Fra Angelico (c. 1387–1455)
Museo di San Marco, Florence, Italy

Known as the Blessed Angelico, he was an Italian monk who used his art to teach others. Fra Angelico painted altarpieces and religious scenes for chapels and convents. In his own monastery he made 50 wall paintings, called frescoes. These were mostly in the cells of the monks to aid them in their silent thoughts and prayers.

Index

highlights
intense
radiant
watery
ultraviolet
wintry
shadowy
mysterious
mottled
slanted
lamplight
dusky
spooky
patterned
blurry
streaky
patchy
nightlight
subdued
bright
pale
spotlight
romantic
guiding
lowlights
laser
blazing
piercing
firelight
fluorescent
harsh
starlight
luminous
floodlight
vivid
infrared

romantic

shadowy

mysterious

ultraviolet

radiant

laser

fluorescent

piercing

subdued

starlight

wintry

blazing

dusky

mottled

spooky

guiding

highlights

blurry

slanted

luminous

vivid

infrared

lamplight

floodlight

bright

nightlight

streaky

firelight

patterned

lowlights

patchy

harsh

spotlight

pale

intense

watery